Simply Dance

Jive and Street Dance

Rita Storey

W

FRANKLIN WATTS
LONDON • SYDNEY

Before you start

Dancing is a great way to get fit and meet people. Wherever you live there are likely to be dance classes held somewhere nearby. There are some steps in this book that you can try to get you started. There are also some suggestions for clips of music to listen to on pages 28–9.

You do not need a special costume to learn to dance. A pair of comfortable shoes and clothes that let you move easily will be fine to start with. It is not a good idea to wear trainers when you are dancing the jive as the soles grip the floor and make it difficult to turn your feet easily. Some dance studios have their own dress code, so you might want to check what it is before turning up to a class.

When you are dancing it is a good idea to wear two or three thin layers of clothing. At the start of a dance session you need to keep your muscles warm to avoid damaging them when you stretch. As you get warmer you can take off some layers.

Like any type of physical exercise, dance has an element of risk. It is advisable to consult a healthcare professional before beginning any programme of exercise, particularly if you are overweight or suffer from any medical conditions. Before you begin, prepare your body with a few gentle stretches and exercises to warm you up.

Dancing is getting more and more popular. Give it a try and find out why!

First published in 2010 by
Franklin Watts
338 Euston Road
London NW1 3BH

Franklin Watts Australia
Level 17/207 Kent Street
Sydney NSW 2000

© Franklin Watts 2010
Series editor: Sarah Peutrill
Art director: Jonathan Hair

Series designed and created for Franklin Watts
by Storeybooks
Designer: Rita Storey
Editor: Nicola Barber
Photography: Tudor Photography

A CIP catalogue record for this book is available from the British Library

Printed in China

Dewey classification: 793.3'3
ISBN 978 0 7496 9365 7

Picture credits
All photographs Tudor Photography, Banbury, unless otherwise stated. © Anky10 Dreamstime.com p14; Michael Ochs Archives/Getty Images p4; Ferdaus Shamim/WireImage p26; © Alan Pappe /Corbis p15; Shutterstock pp 26, 28 and 29; i-stock p16.

Cover images Tudor Photography

All photos posed by models. Thanks to Sam Aires, B-Girl Flex, Ryan Brown, Kimesha Campbell, Micaela Davies, Jordie, Gleanne Purcell-Brown, Emile Ruddock and Libby Williams.

The Publisher would like to thank dance adviser Kate Fisher (www.katefisherdanceacademy.com) for her invaluable help and support.

Franklin Watts is a division of Hachette Children's Books, an Hachette UK company
www.hachette.co.uk

Contents

Ballroom dances

Ballroom dances are performed by couples and recognised in competitions around the world. They are split into two groups: 'International Standard' and 'International Latin'. In International Standard ballroom dancing, a couple must remain in a closed hold (facing each other, with both hands in contact) for most of the dance. Latin dances usually have a lot of hip action and rhythmic expression. They do not always have to be danced in a closed hold. The two partners in a couple may dance side-by-side, or even dance different moves from each other. The jive is a fast, fun International Latin dance.

Street dance

Street dance has its own competitions. There are also classes where you can learn steps and routines. But the great thing about street dance is that you can just get a few mates together, put on some music and dance!

What is the jive?

The history of the jive begins in the dance clubs of New York City in the 1920s and '30s, where new types of music called jazz and swing had become popular. This music was perfect for energetic dances such as the lindy hop **and the** jitterbug.

GI invasion

During the Second World War (1939–45) more than one-and-a-half million US servicemen, known as GIs, came to Great Britain. The GIs brought with them the lindy hop and jitterbug.

The original jitterbug danced in the USA had some very athletic moves. The jitterbug, and lots of variations of it, are still danced today.

These energetic and **acrobatic** dances were completely new to the people of Great Britain. They gradually developed into a dance known as the jive.

GB jive

The style of jive danced in the 1940s in Great Britain was simpler than the original American dances. But although it had fewer acrobatic moves it was still fast and exciting to dance.

Young people loved the jive as it gave them an opportunity to have fun and to forget about the war for a short time.

In 1945, at the end of the war, the GIs left Great Britain – but the jive stayed. Eventually it changed so that it could be danced to a new music craze called **rock and roll**.

Jive styles

The word jive now refers to all the dances that were adapted from the lindy hop and jitterbug.

There are a lot of different variations of the jive and there are classes available in many of them. You can learn French-style **LeRoc**, **Ceroc**, **East Coast Swing**, **West Coast Swing** as well as the original lindy hop and jitterbug. The International Latin jive taught at most dance schools is a mixture of many of these styles. The jive has been standardised so that the same steps are taught in dance schools all over the world.

This couple are dancing an energetic jive.

Jive – the basics

The jive is a fast and energetic dance. Because of the speed of the moves it is important to keep the steps controlled. Learn them at a slow pace and speed them up gradually.

Counting the steps

The basic count for a jive is: one, two, one 'a' two, one 'a' two. The 'a' is a very quick count.

Rock step

The most important step to learn for the jive is the **rock step**. Once you have mastered this

KEY

G   The girl's steps

B   The boy's steps

'count'   Count the moves as you dance them. You can count out loud at first if it helps.

Rock step

one

1 Step back on to your right foot.

1 Step back on to your left foot.

two

2 Transfer your weight back on to your left foot.

2 Transfer your weight back on to your right foot.

step you will have the basis for dancing a jive properly. The back rock step is danced at the beginning of most steps to the count of one, two.

Basic step

The basic step in jive is a rock step followed by a *chasse* to the left and then to the right (boy). The girl dances the opposite steps starting with a rock step back on the right foot.

Jive hold

In an International Latin jive the couple can dance facing their partner, with both hands in contact (**ballroom** or **closed hold**). They can also dance with one hand in contact (**single** or **open hold**).

This couple are in a single (or open hold) dancing a jive.

Chasse to the left

one

'a'

1 Take a small step to the side on your right foot.

1 Take a small step to the side on your left foot.

a Close left foot to right foot.

a Close right foot to left foot.

two

2 Take a small step to the side on your right foot.

2 Take a small step to the side on your left foot.

Then dance a *chasse* to the right by doing the three steps on this page again, but this time changing all the lefts to rights, and all the rights to lefts.

Count one 'a' two

Unlike some ballroom and Latin dances that cover the whole dance floor, the jive is done almost in one spot. The centre of the dance is the handhold and the dance revolves around it.

Keep it light

When you have learned the steps and are performing the jive at speed you will need to dance on the balls of your feet.

Change of place – left to right

one

two

'a'

1 Take a small step to the side with your right foot.

1 Take a small step to the side with your left foot.

a Close left foot to right foot.

a Close right foot to left foot.

2 Take a small step to the side with your right foot and start to turn.

2 Take a small step to the side with your left foot.

one

1 Step to the side with your left foot while turning right.

1 Step to the side with your right foot.

'a'

a Close right foot to left foot, still turning right.

a Close left foot to right foot.

two

2 Facing your partner, take a small side step with your left foot.

2 Facing your partner, take a small side step with your right foot.

one

Finish the move with a rock step like the one on page 6.

1 Step back on to your right foot.

1 Step back on to your left foot.

two

2 Transfer your weight on to your left foot.

2 Transfer your weight on to your right foot.

Steps continue on page 10.

Continue from the rock step on page 9.

American spin

one

'a'

a Close left foot to right foot.

a Close right foot to left foot.

1 Take a small step to the side on your right foot.

1 Take a small step to the side on your left foot.

The American spin

In an **American spin** the girl spins on one foot through one complete turn. As she spins she does not hold on to her partner. It is his job to help her by giving her hand a gentle push to start the turn, and by catching her hand as she completes the turn to help her balance.

two

2 Step on to your right foot and spin all the way round to face your partner.

2 Take a small step to the side on your left foot.

Dance halls

In the 1940s, not many people had television sets – and there were no computer games. For entertainment people listened to the radio, went to the movies or danced. Dance played a very important part in the social lives of young and old alike. All towns and villages had at least one dance hall where people got together, particularly on Friday and Saturday nights, to dance and have fun.

Many dance halls had live music, played by dance orchestras. These ranged from small ensembles with seven instruments to big bands in the large halls.

In some dance halls the jive was banned. It was frowned upon as it was thought to spoil the progress of 'proper' dancers doing the waltz or quickstep.

one

1 Take a small step to the side on your left foot.

1 Take a small step to the side on your right foot.

'a'

a Close right foot to left foot.

a Close left foot to right foot.

two

2 Take a small step to the side on your left foot.

2 Take a small step to the side on your right foot.

Putting it together

The dance steps on pages 6–11 can be joined together to make a routine if you follow the sequence shown below.

Rock step (page 6)

one

two

Chasse to left (page 7)

one

'a'

two

Chasse to right

Then dance a *chasse* to the right by doing the three steps of *chasse* to the left again, but this time changing all the lefts to rights, and all the rights to lefts.

Count one 'a' two

Change of place – left to right (pages 8–9)

one

'a'

two

one

'a'

two

one

two

American spin (pages 10–11)

'a'

one

two

two

one

'a'

Then start the routine again from the beginning.

Competition jive

The steps of the jive are set down in a syllabus that you can learn in dance classes and perform in competitions. The syllabus for a jive makes interesting reading as it includes steps with names such as 'throwaway', 'chicken walks' and 'arm breaker'!

Latin or ballroom

The jive is danced as one of the International Latin dances even though it is not Latin in origin. It used to be danced as a ballroom dance, and the **tango** as a Latin dance, but some years ago they were swapped. The tango is now an International Standard ballroom dance and the jive has moved into the Latin section.

The jive is the last dance to be performed in competitions as it is the fastest and most exhausting.

Judging the jive

A good jive should be very energetic but also neat and controlled. There should be a bouncy action in the knees and feet. The knees are kept close together and the steps include kicks (from the hip) and flicks (from the knee). Both of these moves should finish with pointed toes aimed towards the ground. The jive does not have the high lifts that you see in rock and roll dancing – it is all performed on the floor.

Costumes for dancing the jive

A lot of the movement in the jive is in the legs and feet, so girls' costumes are usually short to show off the footwork. A skirt or fringing that flare out to show off fast spins are both popular.

The jive is a fun dance. Wear something bright, get up on your toes and – most of all – enjoy yourself!

Show dances

In competitions the dancers must follow the rules set down for each dance. If they don't they lose points from their scores. But dances performed for an audience rather than in a competition can break the rules and use exaggerated and dramatic **choreography**. These dances are called show dances. A show jive includes lots of high lifts and acrobatic moves.

Jive in the movies

The movie industry in the 1930s and '40s was dominated by American films. Most of the dance movies of this time feature the American versions of the jive, the lindy hop and the jitterbug.

The Lindy Hoppers appeared in many films, including the 1941 comedy classic *Hellzapoppin'*. This film contains arguably the greatest lindy hop/jitterbug/jive routines ever included in a movie. It includes lots of acrobatic moves, called air steps.

To dance the jive, it was necessary to have a partner. Those without a partner could join in by doing hand movements to the music. This was called a hand jive. The movie *Grease* (1978), starring Olivia Newton-John and John Travolta, features a dance called 'Born to Hand Jive' which has lots of hand jive moves.

The film that showcased the change from jive to rock and roll was *Rock Around the Clock* (1956), starring Bill Haley. The film had a hit record of the same name.

John Travolta (Danny) and Olivia Newton-John (Sandy), dance 'Born to Hand Jive' in the movie *Grease*.

What is street dance?

Street dance is any style of improvised dance that has developed in places such as clubs, playgrounds or on the street. The style of street dance that most people recognise today has evolved from some of the street dance styles that began in the USA in the 1970s and '80s.

A youth culture

Hip hop is a term that covers not only street dance but a whole youth culture. It began in the 1970s in the Bronx, a poor area of New York City in the USA. The young people of this area were mainly African-American or Puerto Rican. DJs such as Afrika Bambaataa and Grandmaster Flash used vinyl records on mixing decks to create a new type of music. A new dance style also evolved, called **b-boying** or **breakdancing**.

B-boying is a mixture of acrobatic head and hand-spins and fast footwork. It was influenced by **martial arts** such as **capoeira** and **kung fu**, as well as the dance moves of singer James Brown.

The dancers formed gangs, called crews, and held breakdance battles. The dances were improvised and the audience reaction selected the winner.

Music and dance were only part of the hip hop scene. Rapping (a rhythmic way of saying words to a beat), **graffiti** art and clothing also played a part in creating a complete lifestyle. The clothing style was urban and edgy. Baggy tops and hoodies were part of the image.

Hip hop has its own style of clothes, music and graffiti art.

Hip hop today

Hip hop was originally linked to 'gangsta' culture, and some still is, but today a new less aggressive style has also gained a wider appeal. This style of hip hop dance is still sharp and strong and danced with a confident attitude but it has lost some of its more confrontational elements.

Street dance styles

Other street dance styles developed in other parts of the USA in the 1970s and '80s. They included **popping**, **locking** and **house dance**.

There are no strict rules in street dance and because of this it can constantly change. While the original styles of street dance are all still popular, other forms have grown up alongside them. Street dance styles are now all loosely refered to as hip hop.

Street jazz

Street jazz – a mixture of jazz dance and street dance, has carefully choreographed moves and is now regularly taught in dance schools.

Krumping

A recent street dance style called krumping is a non-violent alternative to street violence. It can sometimes look like a fight as it involves physical contact between the dancers.

Street jazz is taught in dance schools. It uses the urban, edgy moves of street dance in choreographed routines.

Graffiti

Graffiti is words or pictures written or drawn on walls, buses, trains and in other public places. It is the visual part of hip hop culture. In the 1970s graffiti drawings, called 'tags', were used by street gangs in New York to mark their territory. The tags gradually became larger, more colourful and more elaborate. Graffiti has been elevated to an art form by some talented artists. But there is an ongoing debate about whether most graffiti is art – or simply vandalism.

Street dance – the basics

The first rule of street dance is that it has no rules. Unlike other forms of dance, there is no right or wrong in street dance. The only things that matter are how the dancers feel and the response from the audience.

1 Starting position.

Legs as straight as you can manage.

2 Neutral position.

Jump down, knees bent and together.

Arms out straight, both hands making a fist.

On the balls of your feet.

3 Knees out to make a straight line, arms making a diagonal.

Straight arms.

Hands making a fist.

Knees as clos making a stra line as you c

4 Neutral position.

5 Swivel your feet, moving your left foot out.

6 Neutral position.

How to begin a hip hop routine

First find a piece of music to dance to. There are some suggestions on page 29. Then watch and learn. If there is video of the track, watch the routine and pick out moves you like. Put together steps to fit your music. Do not make your routines too complicated at first. Danced well, a simple routine like the one shown here will look more effective than a very complicated one danced badly.

There are some suggestions on page 29.

Street dance tip

Hip hop steps do not glide from one to the other. Each move must make a strong, separate shape. Look in a mirror as you dance and practise, practise, practise!

7 Same as move 3 but using opposite arms.

8 Neutral position.

9 Same as move 5 but to the other side.

10 Finishing position. Same as position 1 but using opposite arms.

Street dance steps

I n some hip hop moves you use one part of the body while keeping the rest still. These moves are called body isolations.

The snake

In this move the legs are kept still while the upper body moves. It should feel as though you are ducking under an imaginary wire.

The snake

1 Starting position. Legs straight, feet apart.

Bend your right knee.

2 Bend from the waist until your head and the top half of your body are almost parallel to the floor.

3 Keep the bottom half of your body still. Start to straighten up moving first your head, then your shoulders.

1 Finish back in position 1, then repeat moves 2 and 3 to the left.

Keep it sharp

Hip hop routines are even more fun to make up when there are a few of you dancing together. If you use clever but simple choreography you can create routines that even inexperienced dancers can dance well. The key to making a routine look good is getting everyone to move together.

Tip

If you are teaching a routine to a group of dancers, do it in stages. Get them to practise the first few steps at a walking pace, then dance the steps to the music. Keep doing this, adding on a few more steps each time until you have built up the whole routine.

1 Starting position: legs straight, feet apart. Bend forwards from the waist so that your hands are close to the floor. Make your hands into a fist.

2 Lift your left elbow and turn out your left heel.

3 Same as starting position 1.

4 Repeat move 2 but move your right elbow and heel.

You could turn your head as you lift your elbow.

5 Repeat moves 1–4 but this time move opposite heels and shoulders to your partner.

Downrock – six step

1 Crouch down with your hands flat on the floor. Extend your right leg out behind you.

2 Sweep your right leg out to the side.

3 Continue to sweep your right leg round to the front. Take your hands off the floor as your leg moves round.

4 Put your right hand back on the floor. Sweep your right leg round to the left.

5 As your right leg continues to sweep round put both hands back on the floor in front of you.

6 Jump your left leg over your right leg and take your right leg to the back to start again.

Breakdancing moves

The steps on these pages are from breakdancing but are regularly included in hip hop dance routines. Originally breakdancing was made up of four types of step:

toprock – steps danced standing up

downrock – moves done on the floor

power moves – athletic downrock moves such as head-spins

freezes – the final move of a routine (usually a balance) that is held without moving for several seconds.

Balances or freezes

Freezes can be used to end a hip hop dance. Before a freeze, crouch down with your hands on the floor in front of you. Then gently move into a balance and hold it in place for several seconds. These are difficult moves to do, so be very careful. If it starts to hurt, stop straight away.

Freezes

Putting it together

The way you put steps together in street dance is completely up to you. The sequence below is just a suggestion. It can be re-ordered and added to so that it fits the piece of music you have chosen for your dance.

11

12

13

14

15

16

17

18

19

20

21

Then start the routine again from the beginning.

Competition street dance

Street dance competitions are increasingly popular today. National, European and World Street Dance Challenges are all held, as well as many more local competitions.

Hip hop competitions

B-boy (b-girl for girls) and breakdancing crews are battling it out across the world. The 'battle of the year' is an annual competition that features the most innovative international b-boy crews. It also showcases hip hop culture in all its forms.

Street dancers can enter competitions as crews, **solo**, **duos**, **quads** and teams. They can compete at different levels, from newcomer (someone who has never danced in a competition before) to advanced, which is for previous winners and dance teachers.

Whatever style of hip hop is your favourite, you can be sure that there is a competition somewhere for you to enter.

In 2009, the street dance group Diversity wowed voters to win the top prize in the television show *Britain's Got Talent*.

The pictures above show two b-boy or breakdancing power moves. The one on the left is called a windmill, the one on the right a flare.

What do the judges look for?

Judges look for a good range of moves as well as style, timing and lots of confidence.

In b-boying or breakdancing, the judges expect to see dramatic power moves (for example, head-spins, flares and windmills) and a range of freezes.

Street dance competitions often go on for two days. As well as being spectacular dance events they usually include workshops and exhibition dances to help you improve your skills.

Street dance in the movies

In the 1980s breakdance battles, and the crews that danced them, inspired movies such as *Wild Style* (1983), *Flashdance* (1983) and *Beat Street* (1984). Some movies starred the actual crews that featured in the stories. At the time it was almost impossible to find professional dancers to breakdance as well as they could.

You Got Served (2004): A hip hop film about a pair of friends named David and Elgin who want to open their own hip hop dance and recording studio. To make that happen, they must first win a street dance competition.

Save the Last Dance (2001): The story of a young white girl who moves into the ghettos of Baltimore and is introduced to hip hop culture.

Step Up (2006) and *Step Up 2: The Streets* (2008) (PG 13) : Both films follow the stories of students at the Maryland School of the Arts and their love of street dance.

Dance to the music

The music you dance to is very important. The regular beat, or pulse, of the music gives you the timing to move to. The rhythm and feel of the piece help you to perform the dance correctly.

Music for the jive

Jive can be danced to a range of up-tempo music including **boogie-woogie**, jazz and **swing**. This type of music is often played by **big bands**.

Swing music has a happy, upbeat sound. It fits perfectly with the energetic steps of the jive.

Dance music Jive

A list of jive music can be found on: www.dancesportmusic.com/jive.html

Short clips for you to listen to: www.ballroomdancers.com/Music/ search_style.asp?Dance=Jive

Other suggestions are:
'Wake Me Up Before You Go-Go', Wham!
'Reach', S Club 7
'Route 66', John Mayer
'Diamond Light Boogie', Cherry Poppin' Daddies
'Candyman', Christina Aguilera
'Bubble Pop Electric', Gwen Stefani
'Rockin' Robin', Jackson 5
'Happy Birthday Sweet Sixteen', Neil Sedaka
'Oh! Carol', Paul Anka
'Sultans of Swing', Dire Straits

Hip hop DJs are an important part of hip hop culture. As well as playing hip hop music they also create their own sounds.

In the mood

Dancing the jive to swing music helps to recreate the feel of the period in which the dance originated. Some people dress in 1940s-style clothes to help get them in the right mood.

Music for hip hop

There are no strict rules to limit what type of music you can dance hip hop to. Pure street dance is **improvised** (made up as you dance). This means that you can fit the steps to any music with a strong urban sound.

Street dance and jazz routines are taught in dance schools to any popular music with a strong beat. If you want to learn to breakdance, then try dancing to some **rap music**.

Dance music
Street dance

'Uprock', Rock Steady Crew
'Cold Hearted', Paula Abdul
'U Make Me Wanna', Usher
'Love Game', Lady Gaga
'I'm a Slave 4 U', Britney Spears
'Tearin' Up My Heart', *NSYNC
'Wall To Wall', Chris Brown
'Vogue', Madonna
'Planet Rock', Afrika Bambaataa &
the Soulsonic Force
'Peace, Unity, Love and Having Fun',
Afrika Bambaataa
'Don't Stop the Roc', Freestyle
'Scorpio', Grand Master Flash
or dance to any rapping track by Dizzee
Rascal or Eminem

Glossary

acrobatic Describes spectacular moves such as lifts and spins.

American spin A move in jive where the girl spins on one foot through one complete turn.

big band A large group of musicians (typically between 12 and 25) playing trumpets, trombones, saxophones, electric guitar, piano, double bass and drums. Some big bands also have singers.

body isolation Moving one part of the body separately from the rest of the body.

boogie-woogie A form of fast-tempo jazz music.

breakdancing (also called **b-boying**) An early form of street dance influenced by martial arts such as capoeira and kung fu. The moves included acrobatic head and hand-spins and fast footwork.

capoeira An African-Brazilian art form that combines unarmed combat, music and dance.

Ceroc A French-style adaptation of the lindy hop.

chasse A step in which one foot chases the other: step, close, step, close.

choreography The arrangement and sequence of steps that form a dance.

closed hold (also called **ballroom hold**) A dance hold in which the two partners in a couple face each other and keep both hands in contact.

downrock Breakdance moves that are performed on the floor.

duo Two people performing together.

East Coast Swing A dance that evolved from the lindy hop.

freeze The final move of a street dance routine (usually a balance) that is held without moving for several seconds.

graffiti Words or pictures written or drawn on walls, buses, trains and in other public places.

hip hop A term that describes a youth culture that includes street dance.

house dance A street dance style developed in the 1980s.

improvised Describes something that is made up on the spot.

jazz A type of music that developed in the USA in the 1920s and '30s.

jitterbug A dance done to swing music.

kung fu A Chinese martial art.

LeRoc A French-style adaptation of the lindy hop.

lindy hop A dance done to swing music It was named after the US pilot Charles Lindbergh.

locking A hip hop dance style in which the arms and hands are locked and released to create a jerky dance.

martial art A fighting sport that originated in combat or self-defence.

open hold (also called **single hold**) When a couple dance with one hand in contact.

popping A hip hop dance style in which the joints are frozen for a moment then released.

power moves Athletic breakdance moves such as head-spins.

pulse A regular heart beat.

quads Four people performing together.

rap music A type of African-American music in which rhyming lyrics are spoken to a musical accompaniment.

rock and roll A style of music and dance that developed out of swing music and jive dance.

rock step A basic step in a jive dance.

solo One person performing alone.

street jazz A mixture of jazz dance and street dance. It has choreographed moves and is taught in dance schools.

swing A type of popular dance music based on jazz and played by big bands.

syllabus A summary of all the steps you need to learn for each dance medal or grade.

tango A ballroom dance that is Latin-American in origin.

toprock Breakdance moves that are danced standing up.

West Coast Swing A dance that evolved from the lindy hop.

Further information

Websites

Steps to follow and lots of information about ballroom dances at:
www.ballroomdancers.com

UK news and events, region by region, for jive, swing, lindy hop, LeRoc and Ceroc:
www.uk-jive.co.uk/

The official governing body of streetdance in the UK:
www.streetdanceinternational.com/

A site run for and by the Street Dance community:
www.streetdancers.co.uk/

For action from the popular TV dance shows see:
www.bbc.co.uk/strictlycomedancing/
abc.go.com/shows/dancing-with-the-stars
www.fox.com/dance

Dance classes

Find a dance class wherever you are in the world:

www.dancesport.uk.com/studios_world/index.htm

Note to parents and teachers

Every effort has been made by the Publishers to ensure that these websites are suitable for children, that they are of the highest educational value, and that they contain no inappropriate or offensive material. However, because of the nature of the Internet, it is impossible to guarantee that the contents of these sites will not be altered. We strongly advise that Internet access is supervised by a responsible adult.

Index